CONNECTICUT

A PHOTOGRAPHIC CELEBRATION

compiled by the staff of
American Geographic Publishing

MARY ANN BROCKMAN

Above: At work high above downtown Hartford.
Right: Canoeing the Housatonic at West Cornwall.
Facing page: Stonington harbor.

Title page: Port Harbor at Mystic. DAVID KREIDER/PHOTO AGORA

Front cover: Ferry on the Connecticut River seen from
Gillette Castle State Park. MARY ANN BROCKMAN

Back cover, top: Aboard the Charles W. Morgan, an 1841
whaling bark at Mystic Seaport. MARY ANN BROCKMAN
Bottom: The Nathan Hale Homestead at Coventry. JIM CRONK

2

JOHN J. SMITH

ISBN 0-938314-72-6

© 1989 American Geographic Publishing
P.O. Box 5630, Helena, MT 59604
(406) 443-2842

William A. Cordingley, Chairman
Rick Graetz, Publisher & CEO
Mark O. Thompson, Director of Publications
Barbara Fifer, Production Manager

Design by Linda Collins
Printed in Korea by Dong-A Printing through Codra Enterprises,
Torrance, California.

American Geographic Publishing is a corporation for publishing
illustrated geographic information and guides. It is not associated
with American Geographical Society. It has no commercial or
legal relationship to and should not be confused with any other
company, society or group using the words geographic or
geographical in its name or its publications.

KEN LAYMAN/PHOTO AGORA

3

TOM TILL

Above: The Wadsworth Atheneum, Hartford.

Facing page: In Rocky Glen State Park, western Connecticut.

Overleaf: The Port of New London.

J.A. SAWYER

JAN DOYLE

8

Above: *The joys of springtime.*
Right: *Rural living at Granby.*

ROBERT WINSLOW

Above: Sorry, no lottery tickets just now.
Facing page: Up and away in the skies over Meriden.

ROBERT WINSLOW

MARY ANN BROCKMAN

Above: The Henry Whitfield house at Guilford, dating from 1639, is New England's oldest stone dwelling.

Left: Long Island Sound at Hammonasset Beach State Park.

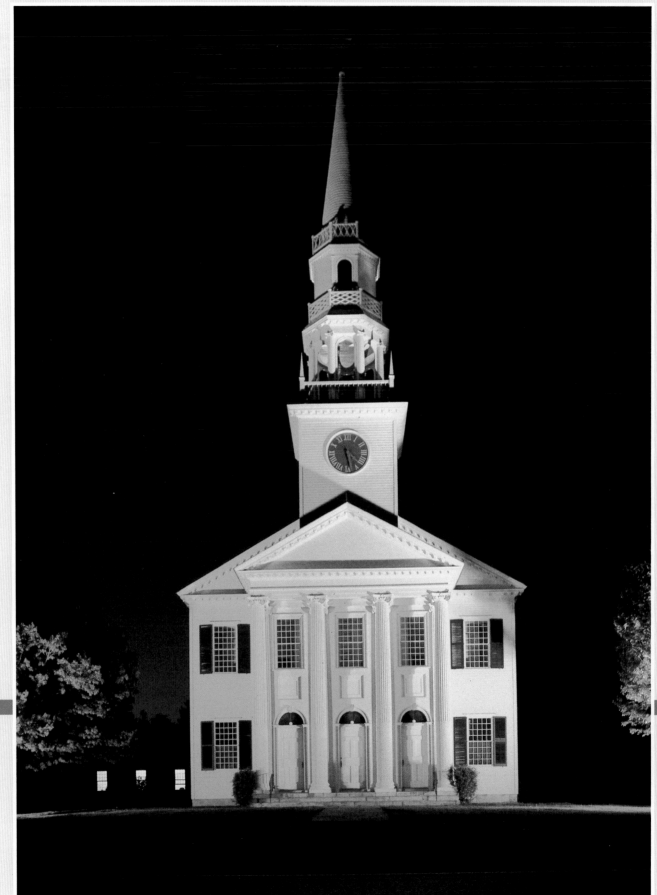

MARY ANN BROCKMAN

JEFF GREENBERG

Right: At Salisbury.
Above: New London business confer-
ence.

Facing page: Litchfield's 1829
Congregational Church.

Overleaf: The Old State House,
Hartford.

15

ERNEST J. LARSEN, JR.

ERNEST J. LARSEN, JR.

ERNEST J. LARSEN, JR.

ROBERT WINSLOW

Left: Autumn silhouettes.
Above: A friendly game at New Haven.

Facing page: Lake Waramang, New Preston.

MAE SCANLAN

MARY ANN BROCKMAN

20

Above: Between Woodbury and Roxbury in the western uplands.
Right: The Mianus River at Greenwich.

DALE C. SPARTAS

21

TOM TILL

Above: *A wintry morning at aptly-named Rocky Neck State Park.*
Right: *Tugboat at Stamford harbor on the Sound.*

Overleaf: *Sundown over Candlewood Lake in western Connecticut.*

DALE C. SPARTAS

24

MARY ANN BROCKMAN

C.A. SCHMEISER/UNICORN

DALE C. SPARTAS

27

Above: *Winter is coming.*
Left: *A pause on the trip south.*

DUANE V. GAMBLE

JAN DOYLE

Above: Invitation on a summer afternoon.
Left: The Harrison House in Branford, which dates from about 1700.

Facing page: Carefully dressed for a powwow.

JAN DOYLE

30

Above: *Reflecting history.*

Facing page: *The Connecticut Capitol, Hartford.*

Overleaf: *A modern office building catches the image of Hartford's Center Church (1807).*

MARY ANN BROCKMAN

34

MAE SCANLAN

DUANE V. GAMBLE

JOHN J. SMITH

35

Right: *Bloodroot.*

Above: *A Revolutionary War re-enactment at Madison.*

Facing page: *At Old Lyme.*

36

JAN DOYLE

Above: *Winter textures.*
Left: *Sheffield Island at Norwalk.*

MARY ANN BROCKMAN

Above: Riverton's Hitchcock Chair Factory, still in use, dates
from 1826.
Facing page: First Presbyterian Church, Stamford.

JEFF GREENBERG

MARY ANN BROCKMAN

JAN DOYLE

Left: Between Milford and Southbury in western Connecticut.

Above: Strawberry time.

MARY ANN BROCKMAN

MARY ANN BROCKMAN

Right: *A graceful beauty at Norwalk.*
Above: *Ready for a kayak race on the Housatonic at West Conwall.*

Facing page: *High-rise living in fast-growing Stamford.*

MAE SCANLAN

DALE C. SPARTAS

MAE SCANLAN

Above: *Autumn blazes at New Preston.*
Facing page: *Riverside Harbor.*

JIM CRONK

JAN DOYLE

Left: *Interesting in joining the team? At Yale.*
Above: *Yale's Sterling Memorial Library.*

Facing page: *Despite the sunlight, feel the nip in the air.*

DALE C. SPARTAS

MARY ANN BROCKMAN

48

Above: Coffee beans plain and fancy at Hadlyme.
Right: The Phoenix Life Building, Constitution Plaza, Hartford.

ERNEST J. LARSEN, JR.

MAE SCANLAN

DUANE V. GAMBLE

C.A. SCHMEISER/UNICORN

Left: *Enjoying Stony Creek at Branford.*
Above: *At Mystic.*

Facing page: *After mass at Christ the King Church, Old Lyme.*

Overleaf: *Tranquil Hamburg Cove at Lyme.*

CHRIST THE KING CHURCH

MASS
SUN. 8:30 10:30
SAT. VIGIL 5:00
E. THRU FRI. 8:00 A.M.
TEL. 434-1669

MARY ANN BROCKMAN

53

54

C.A. SCHMEISER/UNICORN

Above: *Thimble Islands in the morning, Branford.*

Right: *Near Meriden.*

ERNEST J. LARSEN, JR.

58

ERNEST J. LARSEN, JR.

Above: *Taking off from Plantsville.*

Facing page: *Tying up at day's end, Stony Creek.*

ERNEST J. LARSEN, JR.

JIM CRONK

Left: *The tiny Rocky Hill Ferry at Glastonbury.*
Above: *Waterbury's village green.*

DALE C. SPARTAS

Above: *No, the one you got last week was nowhere as fine as this fellow.*
Right: *C.H. Dexter & Sons factory (1767) at Windsor Locks.*

MARY ANN BROCKMAN

ROBERT WINSLOW

Right: *So this is how the maple syrup begins.*
Above: *A Norfolk sugarhouse.*

Facing page: *Nature's design amidst maple leaves.*

Overleaf: *Along the Housatonic River.*

JAN DOYLE

65

66

DALE C. SPARTAS

MARY ANN BROCKMAN

Right: *Winter beauty at North Branford.*
Above: *Downtown Greenwich.*

Facing page: *Welcoming antiquers in Essex County.*

JAN DOYLE

70

Above: The Jonathan Trumble house at Lebanon.
Right: In Nipmuck State Forest.

MARY ANN BROCKMAN

JEFF GREENBERG

Above: *This roof could use just a tad more shine.*

Facing page: *At the Yale Summer Music School, Norfolk.*

DUANE V. GAMBLE

MAE SCANLAN

Above: *A little cautious about visitors, that's all.*
Left: *Coventry herb garden.*

Right: *Handcrafting a boat at Mystic Seaport.*
Above: *The Victorian Gelston Hotel, dating from 1853, at Hadlyme.*

Facing page: *The H.M.S. Rose at Captain's Cove, Bridgeport.*

Overleaf: *The Gold Star Memorial Bridge, Groton.*

DUANE V. GAMBLE

DALE C. SPARTAS

JIM CRONK

Above: Memorial Rose Garden, Norwich.
Left: Lily pads on Florida Pond.

JEFF GREENBERG

JAN DOYLE

Left: *"…my heart with pleasure fills, and dances with the daffodils."* (Wordsworth) **Above:** *A ride backward in time at the Trolley Museum, Branford.*

Facing page: *Historic New London's waterfront.*

JOHN A. SAWYER

JAN DOYLE

Above: *Autumn treats at a roadside stand.*
Right: *Apple trees heavy with the harvest near Wallingford.*

C.A. SCHMEISER/UNICORN

85

DUANE V. GAMBLE

JEFF GREENBERG

JOHN J. SMITH

Above: *A wild geranium in spring.*
Top: *Family day for Cub Scout Pack 43 at Old Furnace State Park, South Killingly.*

Facing page: *Demonstrating the colonial art of cooperage at Ledyard.*

JIM CRONK

Above: Patriot Nathan Hale's homestead, Coventry.

Facing page: Kent Falls—a cool respite on a summer day.

Overleaf: The gentle art of herb-drying at Coventry.

JIM HAMILTON

DUANE V. GAMBLE

MARY ANN BROCKMAN

DUANE V. GAMBLE

Above: enjoying water and shore at Madison
Left: The view of Hartford across the Connecticut from Great River Park.

AND HISTORY

JEFF GREENBERG

JIM CRONK

JEFF GREENBERG

Facing page: Looking past the historic Barnum Institute of Science to the modern Bridgeport Center, downtown Bridgeport.

Above: At Eagleville Dam.
Inset: Swapping stories about the one that...

Overleaf: Classic style at Cornwall.